Baths
of Diocletian

·baths·
·of·diocletian·
guide

Ministero per i Beni
e le Attività Culturali

Soprintendenza Speciale
per i Beni Archeologici
di Roma

Texts by
Matteo Cadario
Nunzio Giustozzi

Electa

Facing title-page
The Octagonal Hall
(formerly a planetarium),
the dome

**Ministero per i Beni
e le Attività Culturali
Soprintendenza Speciale
per i Beni Archeologici
di Roma
Museo Nazionale Romano
alle Terme di Diocleziano**

Soprintendente
Mariarosaria Barbera

Curator
Rosanna Friggeri

Collaboration
Francesca Boldrighini
Carlotta Caruso

*Technical Management
of the Museum*
Marina Magnani Cianetti

*Management
of Promotion Service*
Rosanna Friggeri

Photograph Credits
Archivio Fotografico
Soprintendenza Speciale
per i Beni Archeologici
di Roma
Giorgio Cargnel
Romano D'Agostino
Luciano Mandato
Simona Sansonetti

Published by
Mondadori Electa S.p.A., Milano

www.electaweb.com

Contents

Baths of Diocletian

The historic seat of the National Museum of Rome is located in one of the most important archeological areas in Rome, on which stand the remains of the Baths of Diocletian, the largest in the capital and decorated in a particularly magnificent fashion. The emperor commenced their construction in 298 AD, in the Regio VI, on a site covering more than 32 acres, and the work was concluded in 306, a year after the abdication of Diocletian and his coruler Maximian, under the reign of Galerius and Constantius Chlorus. In the building the scheme of the imperial *thermae* was applied on a monumental scale, with the structures housing the baths proper (arranged in a now established sequence: *natatio, frigidarium, tepidarium, caldarium*) located inside a large enclosure, concluded by an exedra. The baths remained in function until the time of the Byzantine-Gothic war (535-53), when, after the cutting of their aqueducts, they were abandoned and their plundering began. Yet they remained visible right through the Middle Ages and all the way up to the 15th and 16th centuries, when they were studied and drawn by architects and antiquarians and still retained much of their original decoration.

Michelangelo's Cloister, the central fountain.

The major transformation of the complex was carried out at the behest of Pius IV, who between 1561 and 1562 first had the *frigidarium* converted into the basilica of Santa Maria degli Angeli e dei Martiri and then decided to found a Carthusian monastery inside the baths. The design of both buildings was entrusted to Michelangelo (the church would be renovated by Vanvitelli in 1749). The work continued until the end of the 16th century and, in addition to the construction of the church, entailed the building of two cloisters that were inserted into the ancient baths, using part of the existing free spaces. Later on, the installation of the city granaries in the halls of the baths and the construction of the large Villa Montalto Peretti resulted in destruction of more of the old structures.

But the last significant alterations to the complex were not made until after the transfer of the capital of Italy to Rome, when, in addition to the dissolution of the congregation of the Carthusians of Santa Maria degli Angeli e dei Martiri, Palazzo Massimo and the Stazione Termini were constructed, Via Cernaia was opened and Piazza Exedra was laid out. All these interventions entailed the elimination of ancient ruins and in particular what remained of the outer enclosure of the baths.

The surviving Roman buildings, corresponding to the complex of the Charterhouse, began their history as an exhibition space in 1889, the date of the foundation of the National Museum of Rome, opened in 1890. But the opportunity for restoration of the ancient buildings was provided by a major archeological exhibition in 1911, staged to mark the fiftieth anniversary of the unification of Italy. This also allowed the state to take over the parts still in private hands, such as the Octagonal Hall. The work of renewal and then conversion into a museum was concluded in the 1930s, prior to the large-scale reorganization in the 1990s, when the exhibits were shared out amongst the new premises of Palazzo Massimo, Palazzo Altemps, the Crypta Balbi and the Museo Palatino, leaving the epigraphic collections, the protohistoric materials and a significant part of the ancient statuary in the historic seat of the museum.

Hall IX of the baths.

Reconstruction
of the plan of the complex
of Diocletian's Baths.

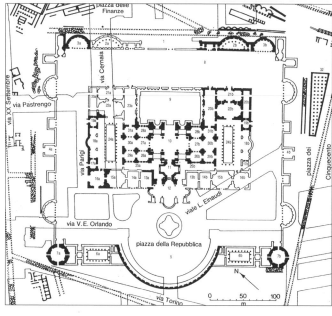

External view of the halls located between the *frigidarium* and the southeastern palaestra.

The Baths of Diocletian today.

External Gardens, 16th-Century Garden and Entrance Hall

The National Museum of Rome is now also responsible for the **External Gardens**, located outside the complex made up of the Cloisters and the Baths of Diocletian, although they contain only a few works. Passing through these gardens from Via De Nicola, enter the **16th-Century Garden**, which has instead been part of the museum since its foundation: the materials located in this garden are chiefly of funerary origin, i.e. statues, stelae, altars and sarcophagi. The center of the garden is occupied by a colossal marble krater, about 2 m high and decorated with a series of erotes from which water spouts. This was in fact the original function of these vases, used as ornaments for gardens and fountains in antiquity.

In the garden are set several statues, both of men (mostly clad in togas) and women (Large and Small Herculaneum types). The toga was the formal dress of the Roman citizen and we can follow the evolution of its drapery over the centuries in these statues. In the entrance stand two statues of children, wearing togas and adorned with *bullae*, amulets that were hung around the neck until the age of 17. Along the path that borders the garden are set funerary stelae, chiefly of soldiers, with two main groups that can be referred to Nero's bodyguard and the praetorians. A series of fine strigilate sarcophagi (i.e. decorated with grooves) can be seen at the rear. From the garden, passing through the ticket office, you come to the Entrance Hall, corresponding to the old passageway of the Carthusian monastery that led to Michelangelo's Cloister. The entrance hall houses several works of value, including a fine sarcophagus decorated with a Dionysiac procession made up of centaurs, satyrs and maenads and a 2nd-century-AD toga-clad statue whose head was replaced in the 4th century by a portrait of Constantius Gallus, brother of Julian the Apostate. (M.C.)

The Entrance Hall.

Krater-fountain at the center
of the 16th-Century Garden.

The Entrance Hall.

Sarcophagus with Dionysiac procession from the area of Santo Stefano Rotondo.

On page 14:
Cinerary altar of the scribe of the curule aediles Quintus Fulvius Priscus and his brother.

The Epigraphic Museum

The Entrance Hall leads to the epigraphic section of the museum, housing one of the most important collections in the world, displayed in a layout that is arranged on three different levels. The term epigraphy refers to the branch of history that studies written texts used for communication that was not private and that was recorded on durable material. The importance of this form of communication in the Roman world is indisputable, even though the phenomenon was increasingly confined to the cities, and to Rome in particular.
The collection allows us to follow the process of evolution from the rare inscriptions of the archaic period to the thousands produced in the imperial age. Each inscription met a twofold need: fixing and handing down a written content, as well as offering a suitable visual presentation of that content.

So examination of an epigraphic document has to be comprehensive, not limited to a reading of the text, but also considering the way in which it has been "made up," the type of support (bronze, stone, plaster, ceramics, etc.) and the technique of writing used. Moreover, epigraphs offer a less exclusive view of the society of the time than do literary sources, as they are an expression of a more diverse range of social classes than the small intellectual elite which has produced most literature. The number of inscriptions on display in the rooms is considerable, and for this reason only the most significant will be mentioned.

Rooms I, II, III and IV

Room I presents the various forms of written communication used by the Romans, showing us the authors of the inscriptions, their contents and the practical aspects of their execution.

Room II is devoted to the earliest examples (9th-6th century BC) that document the progressive adoption of an alphabet to write the Latin tongue: of particular importance is the small vessel found in the necropolis at Osteria dell'Osa, dated to the end of the 9th century BC, which bears the oldest Greek inscription to have been discovered in Italy, a graffito of disputed interpretation, perhaps an exclamation of joy or an allusion to weaving. Inscriptions from the 7th century BC are rare and are mostly linked to the custom of offering gifts to the living or the dead: the texts usually consist solely of the names of the beneficiary and the donor. For the first public epigraphs, used to communicate official texts, usually of a religious character, we have to wait until the archaic period (6th century BC). The room houses a cast of the Forum Cippus (II, 2), a block of tuff found in the area of the Comitium in the Roman Forum, in a shrine located under the black marble paving (*Lapis Niger*) where the original is still located. The text relates part of a sacred law from the monarchic period, containing instructions from the king to a herald. Alongside the cippus are displayed materials from the rich votive deposit connected with the complex. The *Lapis Satricanus*, found in the temple of Mater Matuta at Satricum where it had been reutilized, was originally the base of a donarium containing offerings made by sodales (warriors) loyal to Publius Valerius, identified with Publicola, the first Roman consul elected at the time of the republic's foundation (509 BC). Among the sacred inscriptions it is worth mentioning a sheet of bronze inscribed with a dedication to Castor and Pollux, dated to the second half of the 6th century BC and deposited in the sanctuary of the thirteen altars at Lavinium. From a tomb at Lanuvium comes the fine panoply (helmet and breastplate) (II, 15) of a warrior who combined his military role with a fondness for the Greek culture of the gymnasium, represented by a discus for throwing.

Room III contains materials and inscriptions from the middle republican period (4th-3rd century BC), coming from Rome and the rest of Latium. In this period epigraphs were still fairly few in number, with a marked predominance of those of a sacred character, chiefly dedications and offerings that present a picture of the pantheon of gods worshipped at the time: of particular interest are the small base of a donarium for Aesculapius from the temple on the Isola Tiberina; a limestone crown for the Fortuna Primigenia from

Helmet from the tomb
of the warrior at Lanuvio.

Marble basin of fountain
(*labrum*).

On pages 18-19:
The hall of the Epigraphic
Museum.

the great sanctuary of Praeneste (III, 25); a peperino cippus offered to Aeneas, the Trojan hero venerated at the sanctuary of Lavinium as a Lar, i.e. a deified ancestor. From the sanctuary of Hercules at Borgo San Giovanni, near Lanuvium, comes a marble basin used as a fountain (*labrum*) (III, 8) and inscribed on the lip with a refined technique that involved the use of letters made of metal to compose the epigraph. The text, of official character, records the name of a local aedile who dedicated the monument. The room concludes with the exceptional votive complex of the sanctuary of Demeter and Kore at Aricia (III, 12-16): dating from sometime between the late 4th century BC and the first half of the 3rd, it is made up of three seated statues and two terracotta busts of outstanding importance (see p. 30).

View of the second floor of the Epigraphic Museum.

Room IV is devoted to late-republican inscriptions (2nd-1st century BC) that document the emergence of new social classes in a society engaged in the building and rule of a Mediterranean empire. Found at Fregellae, the inscribed base of Lucius Mummius, consul in 146 BC, is an example of an official and celebratory memorial, but other inscriptions help us to reconstruct the way in which contracts were awarded (IV, 6-7), a process connected with the rise of the equestrian order, and give us an idea of the fierce competiveness of electoral contests, attested by two small bowls inscribed with propaganda relating to L. Sergius Catiline (64 BC) and M. Porcius Cato (IV, 2-3). Simple inscribed cippi (IV, 8-13) as well as reliefs with portraits (IV, 17) from the end of the republican period bear witness to the particularly well-off position in which some freedmen found themselves in an urban setting. Even women, while still confined to a secondary social role, were able to attain a degree of independence from the economic and professional viewpoint, as is demonstrated by the sepulchral inscription dedicated by Eurysaces, a wealthy baker and contractor of the Augustan age, to his wife Antistia, and by the so-called *laudatio Turiae* (IV, 29), a funeral oration carved in marble for a courageous wife who had preserved the family estate at the time of the civil wars and was, according to her husband, a model of feminine virtues throughout forty years of marriage.

Rooms V, VI, VII

The display of epigraphs from the imperial age (1st-4th century AD) commences in the last room on the ground floor: **Room V**, laid out on two floors, illustrates the figure of the emperor and the establishment of the imperial cult.

Recent excavations, carried out on the slopes of the Palatine near the Arch of Constantine, have uncovered an important group of statues from the Augustan and Julio-Claudian dynasties (V, 1-2): the dedication of effigies of members of the imperial family was in fact one of the most common ways of doing it honor. The oldest monument is a base faced in bronze dedicated by the *aenatores* (players of bronze musical instruments), intended to support a portrait statue of Tiberius; the contents of the inscription allow us to date the document to 7 BC. The second monument, again dedicated by the *aenatores*, was carved in marble instead and had a dynastic character: in fact it is a long base (restored during Nero's reign, in the years 55-56

Ulysses and the Sirens,
detail from the sarcophagus
of the eques Marcus
Aurelius Romanus.

Sarcophagus of Julius
Achilleus with pastoral
scenes.

Tabula alimentaria of the
Ligures Baebiani, bronze.

AIANOAVG ... IIII

PACTO

...ATIO PRINCIPIS OBLIGARVNT PRA...

...IN DVLGENTIE EIVS PVERI PVELLE Q... ...IO LIGVRES BAEBIA...

...CIPIANT

AD) on which are inscribed the names of the members of the imperial family portrayed in the statues that were placed on it (Augustus, Claudius, Nero and his mother Agrippina the Younger). The rest of the room is devoted to the compital cult (IV, 3-5) which, from the Augustan age onward, was the principal form in which the citizenry demonstrated their loyalty to the emperor.

On the upper floor are located epigraphs dating from later centuries, including one from AD 196 in which Julia Domna, the wife of Septimius Severus, is given the "military" title of *mater castrorum*, or "mother of the camps" (V, 8).

Room VI, laid out along the two walkways on the right and left of the second floor, sets out to illustrate the stratification of Roman society, presenting on the one on the right the upper classes (the emperor with the imperial family and the senatorial order), and on the one on the left inscriptions connected with the middle classes, including the local class of the *decuriones*, the military, the artisans responsible for large-scale production and the class of powerful imperial freedmen. Among the exhibits are numerous fragments of *fistulae*, lead pipes used for running water: the possibility of obtaining these direct connections to the aqueducts was a privilege reserved for members of the highest classes. The same social classes were frequently proprietors of large factories producing building materials: the numerous fragments of bricks with kiln marks document some of the most important.

The space between the two walkways is dedicated to the equestrian order: in the 3rd-century-AD sarcophagi the figurative decoration is accompanied by an epigraphic account of the dead man's life. The sarcophagus of the young *eques* Marcus Aurelius Romanus (of which only the lid survives, VI, 49) has a complex program of decoration: the portrait of the deceased between two philosophers, a reference to study and culture, is contrasted with the myth of Ulysses and the Sirens, indicating that, like the Homeric hero, the young man had spurned the temptations of life. The large sarcophagus with pastoral scenes (VI, 51) records, in its inscription, the career of Julius Achilleus, an imperial functionary who held the post of superintendent at the Ludus Magnus, the great barracks occupied by gladiators in the vicinity of the Colosseum.

Room VII presents epigraphs related to the administration of the empire. The first inscriptions (VII, 1-4) illustrate the traditional *cursus honorum* created in the republican age, i.e. the sequence of public offices in the career of a senator, from minor magistracies to the high posts to which he could aspire after the consulate. In the imperial age new posts were created, such as the *praefectura urbis*, with policing functions and judicial authority (VII, 9), and the *praefectura alimentorum*, to which one of the most important documents in the museum's collection refers, the bronze *tabula alimentaria* of the Ligures Baebiani (VII, 12) recording the measures taken by Trajan on behalf of poor children in AD 101 and aimed at boosting the population of the Ligurian community that had been deported to Samnium as a punishment in the 2nd century BC. Other prefectures represented the apex of the equestrian career, however: that of the *annona*, documented in the slab of G. Junius Flavianus (VII, 14), which ensured

Rome's food supply, while the responsibilities of that of the praetorium included command of the emperor's armed guard (VII, 22).

Rooms VIII, IX, X

In **Room VIII** we find documents relating to economic activities, throwing light on various aspects of commerce, production and handicrafts in the Roman world. The first inscriptions (VIII, 1-5) concern the management and administration of the *horrea*, the great warehouses that were used to store foodstuffs, thereby guaranteeing the capital's food supply (the *annona*). One that stands out is the funerary altar of Aurelia Nais (VIII, 3), a *piscatrix* (fish vendor) who worked in the area now known as Testaccio in the 2nd century AD. A great deal of space is also devoted to individual trades and crafts, both through presentation of the "guilds" (*collegia*) founded by dealers and artisans (like the slab of the unguent and incense vendors, VIII, 10), and through a selection of epigraphs illustrating the career of individual "professionals," such as the urn of Sellia Epyre who made and sold clothing decorated with gold (*auri vestrix*, VIII, 14) or

Iron collar of a slave.

Front of the sarcophagus of Titus Flavius Trophimas with scenes of craftsmen at work.

the cattle merchant M. Antonius Teres (*negotiator*, VIII, 15). Then there are professional entertainers like the celebrated mime L. Aurelius Apolaustus Memphius (VIII, 20), the winner of many dramatic competitions who had been made one of the *decuriones* of Tivoli, and the comic actor (comoedus) P. Vinicius Laces (VIII, 22), as well as reliefs recording the spectacles of gladiators in the amphitheaters (VIII, 24-5). But the Roman economy was also based on slavery, as we are reminded by the inscription on the bronze collar of a slave promising a reward, should he escape, to anyone who brought him back to his master Zoninus (VIII, 38).

With **Room IX** we enter the world of Roman religion: the collection is organized in such a way as to show the remarkable range of choice available, providing that fidelity was displayed to the traditional public cults. However, the exhibits related to private worship have been kept separate from those of a public character, located along with the inscriptions connected with Eastern religions in the room that opens onto Room X. The private forms were primarily household ones, officiated by the *paterfamilias* and venerating the Penates (IX, 1), Lares (IX, 2) and Manes (one thinks of the frequent invocation *Dis Manibus*, IX, 3), the Personal Genius (IX, 2) and, through them, deceased members of the family, whom these deities personified in various ways, thereby providing a structure for ancestor worship, one of the last forms of paganism to vanish. Gods were often represented on funerary stelae as well: for example Mercury appears as the psychopomp, who accompanied the dead to Hades, on the stele erected by Sextius Rufus Decebalus to his son Achilleus (IX, 4). Among the funeral inscriptions are numerous Christian ones, distinguished from their pagan counterparts by their location (the catacombs) and epigraphic formulas: in fact they used distinc-

tive symbols, such as the fish (the Greek word for fish, *ichthys*, is an acrostic of the formula "Jesus Christ, God's son, Savior"), anchor or dove (as on the funerary stele of Licinia Amias, IX, 24), or contained characteristic expressions like *in pace* or *in Christo* (see the slab of Priscus, IX, 29) and were accompanied (or replaced) by figurative decorations with scenes from the Old and New Testament (see the plaque carved with Noah on the Ark, IX, 35) (fig. 14) or Gospel themes, like the image of the Good Shepherd (IX, 36). There was also a flourishing Jewish community in Rome, as is attested by the lid of Faustina's sarcophagus on which the customary decoration of theatrical masks is accompanied by Hebraic symbols (IX, 20): the menorah (seven-branched candelabra), the ritual horn and the palm branch, as well as the Hebrew salutation *shalom* ("peace").

Room IX continues with a space set aside for Eastern religions, housing epigraphs concerning the cults of Isis, Mithras, Sol and Jupiter Heliopolitanus, a deity venerated at a shrine on the Janiculum whose history is reconstructed in the museum. The fine altar of Cantinea Procla (IX, 55) is dedicated to a priestess of Isis (fig. 15), who is portrayed with the symbols of her role (sistrum, lustral vase and wreath of ears of grain). However, the most numerous relics are related to the worship of the sun god Mithras, represented as Petrogenitus in a statuette from the 2nd century AD (IX, 41) and as Tauroctonus in a fine polychrome relief (IX, 39), both from the Mithraeum discovered underneath Santo Stefano Rotondo in Rome.

Among other things, **Room X** houses the recent finds that have made it possible to reconstruct the cult of Anna Perenna. Magical and propitiatory inscriptions, with charms and curses, are documented by *defixiones*, sheets of metal on which the spell was engraved and that were then rolled up and transfixed by nails. (M.C.)

Funerary stele
of Licinia Amias.

Slab carved with the scene
of Noah on the Ark,
taken from Genesis.

Funerary altar
of Cantinea Procla.

Relief with Mithras
Tauroctonus.

Mithras Petrogenitus.

Beautiful Goddesses, in Terracotta

In 1927 workers on a farm at the locality of Casaletto in Valle Ariccia brought to light the remains of a small sanctuary of considerable antiquity, whose votive deposit contained numerous figurative ex-votos, heads of men and women and anatomical offerings. In the sanctuary, an early phase oriented toward the sphere of *sanatio* or healing was followed at the end of the 4th century BC by a "refoundation" which had consequences on the architectural plane as well. To this phase belong the large clay sculptures, "Sicilian" in style, with the *megalai theai* represented in the form of busts, i.e. as they reemerge from the Underworld. The qualifying elements, such as the ears of grain interwoven with the hair or diadem, or the piglet that one of the seated figures held in her hand, point us in the direction of the religious world of Demeter and Kore. The half-length image is also employed to represent Demeter, even though it is specific to Kore/Persephone. In the latter case, in fact, the bust evokes the *anados*, the moment of return in her cyclic rise from the depths of the earth. Although data on the excavation are insufficient, we can imagine that there was a small *naos* inside the precinct, with a platform on which stood the divine busts, ascribable to more than one modeler in clay. An extremely refined sculptor must have been responsible for the more imposing and matronly bust of Demeter/Ceres, which depicts the goddess in majestic serenity and presents the happy ending to the mother's story and Zeus's eternal guarantee of the new order: nature has resumed its cycles of growth, the Great Goddesses protect the annual ripening of the crops and reveal to mortals the secrets of reproduction and the births of men and animals, ensuring the continuity of life. (N.G.)

Woman offering a piglet.

Bust of Demeter.

The Eulogy of *Allia Potestas*

Funeral inscriptions often give information about the life of the deceased, usually in a formal manner but sometimes telling the story of individuals in a more "familiar" way. In 1912 an elegant slab of marble was discovered in the Salario burial ground, near the Via Pinciana, that must have been attached with nails and has been dated to the first half of the 2nd century AD on linguistic grounds. Care was taken over the layout of the text.

The customary formula of dedication to the Manes, *Dis Manib(us)*, is inscribed at the top in larger letters and beneath it is set the name of the deceased, Allia Potestas, freedwoman of Allius. In the two columns underneath are carved the poetic text of her funeral *elogium*, written in hexameters and all of fifty lines long. The last two lines contain an invitation not to profane the grave. The poem is written in a style influenced by Ovid, although its author cannot have been very adept, as he uses a frequently colloquial and occasionally naïve language and sometimes forgets to respect the meter. It is likely that he was Allius, Allia's patron, who speaks in the first person in the poem. In any case he has followed, albeit in his own way, the tradition of the *laudatio funebris*, which was normally split into three parts: the lament over the death, an illustration of the deceased's merits and a description of the grief of those who remain. The first lines, after the unusual reference to the woman's birth at Perugia, contain concepts commonly found in epitaphs: the idea that a small urn is able to contain the body of such a grand woman and the complaint that Persephone and Fate always take the best things away. The description of Allia's qualities is much more original, because in addition to the customary moral virtues (those normally ascribed to the matron) and practical merits, such as skill in weaving, industriousness or an abstinence from gossip, it dwells on her physical traits. Both the length and the wording used are out of the ordinary and suggest an intimate knowledge of the woman on the author's part: he praises her shining eyes, blond hair, breasts, ivory skin and legs, which remind him of those of Atalanta (the swift-footed huntress) in theatrical performances. Perhaps her only defect was her rough hands. The following lines are somewhat enigmatic and praise Allia for having been able to maintain harmony between two young lovers, who behaved like Orestes and Pylades (a celebrated pair of friends in mythology), living peacefully together in the same house as long as Allia was alive, only to grow old separately after her death. It is likely that Allia was the concubine of her grieving patron, while it is not clear who the two young men were, the patron himself and a friend or two other men. In any case the inscription records and commends the woman's polyandry in a surprising way.

The final part of the text is reserved for the grief of the inconsolable patron, who now awaits his own death, wearing a gold bracelet inscribed with Allia's name and adoring her image, which he wants to place in his tomb. The man also asserts that the woman is destined to live forever in his verses and concludes with another expression of pain at his loss. (M.C.)

The eulogy of Allia Potestas.

An Idol for a Secret Ritual

At the beginning of the 20th century the remains of a small shrine dedicated to Syrian deities were found on the southeastern side of the Janiculum: Baal, venerated in Rome as Jupiter Heliopolitanus, and the minor divinities of the Heliopolitan triad: Atargatis (whom the Romans called Syrian Venus) and Simios (Mercury).
It is the last phase of the shrine, dating from the mid-4th century AD, that has been uncovered, and its plan reflects precise ritual requirements. Around a large courtyard, where the worshipers probably gathered, are set two groups of structures: to the west a building with a basilican plan, used for daily rites as is apparent from the marble statue of the god (perhaps Jupiter Heliopolitanus), found in the niche at the rear, and to the east a room with a mixtilinear plan. At the center of the latter stood a triangular altar with a hollow that housed the famous bronze idol, still covered with votive offerings (eggs, flowers, seeds) at the time of its discovery. The small idol represents a male figure, wrapped by seven coils of a snake that allude to the seven celestial spheres, and has been identified as the Egyptian Osiris or the Syrian Adonis, gods who were born and died each year and were both linked with the cycle of the seasons. In order to act out the allegory of the death and rebirth of the god, and therefore of the neophyte before and after initiation, the statuette was periodically taken out of its hiding place, venerated by the priests and worshipers and then put back again until the next ceremony of initiation into the mystery cult. (N.G.)

Photograph taken at the moment of discovery of the altar containing the bronze idol during the excavation carried out by Paul Gauckler (1908-1910). Rome, Via Dandolo, Syrian sanctuary.

A photograph of the idol in the pit taken at the moment of its discovery.

On pages 34-35: Front and back of the Janiculum idol.

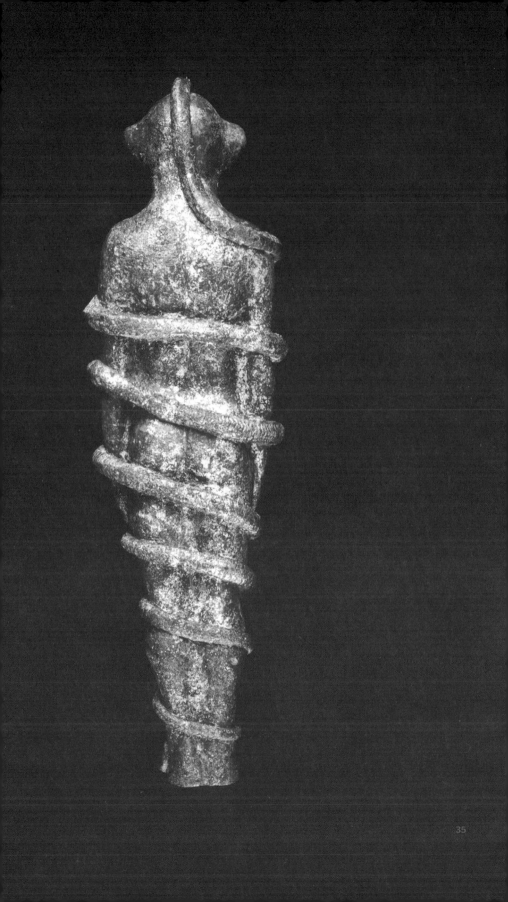

The Protohistoric Museum

The protohistoric section, which is located on the second floor of Michelangelo's cloister and can be reached directly from Room X of the epigraphic museum, illustrates the oldest phases of Latial culture, dating from between the end of the Bronze Age and early Iron Age (11th–10th century BC) and the Orientalizing period (7th–early 6th century BC). The geographical region covered corresponds to ancient Latium (the area to the south of the Tiber), while the materials exhibited all come from verified contexts of excavation and have been chosen in such a way as to reconstruct the social, political and economic organization of the region. The exhibition follows the changes resulting from contact with the Etruscan world and the Greek colonies, present in Campania from the 8th century BC onward. It is split into two parts,

On page 36:
A view of the protohistoric
section of the museum.

Contents of the male
cremation tomb in pit 1,
Quadrato (Rome)
(Latial period I).

the first devoted to a general reconstruction of Latial culture and
the second to individual centers in the region, such as Osteria del-
l'Osa and Fidenae.

Latial Culture

This section sets out to reconstruct the context in which the Latial culture formed and developed, starting out from the organization of the
territory, with the initial dominance of the Alban Hills, central from
the geographical viewpoint as well, which preceded that of the Roman
area, favored by its role as a link between Etruria and Campania (the
birth of Rome is not tackled as this subject has been reserved for the
Museo Palatino). Study of the necropolises has yielded a significant
demographic sample that has permitted reconstruction of the average
age (around 30) and life expectancy of people on the basis of their
social class in the Early Iron Age. The importance of grave goods in
establishing the status of the deceased and thus the organization of
society itself has also been recognized (two cremations of high-ranking
personages from the Forum of Caesar and from Quadrato are on display). Some objects were used as indicators of the deceased's political,

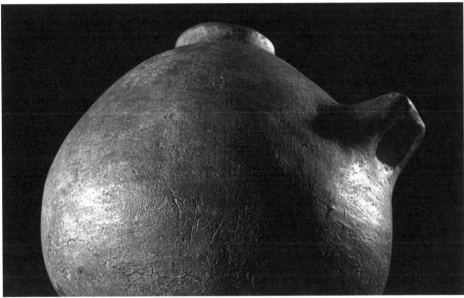

military and religious role and others to distinguish their sex and age. The same period saw a shift from "extended" family groups to the *gens/clientela* structure, which was to survive into archaic Latin society. The Orientalizing period brought a clearer division into social classes, which was associated with the display of inordinate wealth in the tombs of the dominant class. Their contents allow us to follow the development of handicrafts, in ceramics as well as metal, where techniques were improved to meet the ever growing demand for luxury objects from the elites. The presence of imported objects in the tombs reflects the development of external contacts, which in the initial phase were chiefly interregional but progressively expanded to the rest of the Mediterranean world, as can be seen from the Greek inscription found at Osteria dell'Osa, on display in the Epigraphic Section.

Graphic reconstruction of tomb 15 at Castel di Decima, a pit containing a male interment (Latial period IVa).

Flask with Greek inscription from tomb 482 in the necropolis of Osteria dell'Osa.

The Main Centers

Contents of the male cremation tomb in pit 142, necropolis of Osteria dell'Osa (Latial period II).

Grave goods of tomb 32, containing the interment of a child in the necropolis of Castiglione (Latial period II).

This section is devoted to the reconstruction of several important necropolises in the territory of Latium. The most thoroughly investigated is certainly that of Osteria dell'Osa, the place where the Latin city of Gabii would emerge at the end of the 8th century BC and that once faced onto the lake which had formed in the ancient crater of Castiglione. About 450 graves (containing cremations as well as interments), corresponding to extended family groups made up of several dozen members, date from the period comprised between the 10th and 9th century BC (Latial II). The objects deposited in the tombs were already selected in relation to the deceased's role: the spindle whorl, for instance, alludes to the social importance of weaving and is found in women's tombs, while the large *tazza* is typical of the graves of old people, a mark of their control over the distribution of food. Other objects, such as fibulae, give us an insight into dress. The tombs include several male cremations in hut urns. A group of about 65 tombs from between the 9th and 8th

century has been identified that shows the emergence of an aristocratic group separated from the rest of the community. A weapon
appears for the first time in the tomb of an old man and the artifacts
become more specialized. Several tombs from between the second
half of the 8th and the 7th century BC have very rich contents and
one (t. 62) is a joint chamber, and thus was used by the same noble
family. The birth of an aristocratic society is also confirmed by the
presence of many warriors (t. 600 with weapons) and the inclusion
of types of pot that allude to the custom of the banquet, which had
a very important ideological function. The pottery, turned on the
wheel, includes forms of vases inspired by Greek or Phoenician
models. After the tombs from Osteria dell'Osa the partly contempo-
rary necropolis at nearby Castiglione is presented, along with the
excavation of a hut at Fidenae (see p. 42).

Reconstruction of the contents
of a warrior's tomb no. 600
in the necropolis of Osteria
dell'Osa.

Reconstruction of the setting
of the krater at Castiglione.

The Hut at Fidenae

Between 1986 and 1993 a series of excavations conducted at Fidenae, a town on the Via Salaria not far from Rome, led to a discovery that has been of great help in reconstructing the appearance of a settlement at the end of the 9th century BC. Fidenae was an important center in Latium until the 5th century BC, when it was definitively incorporated into Roman territory (426 BC). Permanent occupation of the plain commenced at the beginning of the Iron Age (period IIB), but the excavation has uncovered a slightly later phase (period III) and this has led to the identification of a hut (with an area of about 30 square meters) that had been destroyed by fire. The hut is the type of dwelling that characterizes the protohistoric settlements of Latium.

Reconstruction of the hut at Fidenae.

The museum houses a complete reconstruction of the building at Fidenae, made possible by its excellent state of preservation, and this is accompanied by a significant part of the materials found. The most intriguing of these is the charred skeleton of a feline, evidently killed in the fire, as it is perhaps the earliest evidence for the domestication of cats in Italy. Other reconstructions illustrate various stages in the building of the hut. It has a rectangular plan and the walls were constructed using a particular technique known as *pisé*, which entailed ramming earth mixed with water and straw into a wooden mold. The wall was then reinforced with piles, while four large, upright poles supported the roof. An important element was the bank of tuff and the semicircular row of piles that were erected further up the slope, evidently to protect the entrance of the hut from debris brought down from the top of the hill by erosion. It is likely that the piles came from an older hut and had been reused in the new building. Excavation has also permitted reconstruction of the internal organization of the hut: the hearth, complete with andirons, was located at the center of the room, while on the left of the door, preceded by a hollow used for drainage and covered by a walkway, were found three large *dolia* (food containers) and a small buried pot, implying that this sector was used for storage. The smallest pot held nothing but clay and was probably utilized by the potter. On the opposite side the remains of furniture made out of elm wood suggest that this was where the beds were located, while the floor was of beaten earth. Analysis of the plant remains has identified cereals (spelt, barley) and pulses, while analysis of the animal remains has shown them to belong to sheep, cattle and pigs. (M.C.)

Michelangelo's Cloister

Emerging from the Entrance Hall we come to the Cloister of the Charterhouse of the church of Santa Maria degli Angeli e dei Martiri. The cloister is traditionally attributed to Michelangelo because it was to him that the task of converting the *frigidarium* of the Baths of Diocletian into a church in 1561 had been given. In effect the church and Charterhouse have a coherent design, but it is more likely that Michelangelo (who died in 1564) had merely suggested the layout and then entrusted the job to a pupil, Giacomo del Duca, who was involved in the work in at least the initial phase. This began in 1565 and was not completed until the beginning of 1600. But the second floor of the cloister was only finished in 1676 and the fountain that stands at the center of the garden was built in 1695. The models applied

On page 44:
Michelangelo's cloister.

Views of Michelangelo's
cloister.

in the cloister are those of Carthusian architecture, adapted to the Roman style of architecture of the late 16th century. The complex, which had undergone various alterations over the course of the centuries, was restored for the Jubilee of 2000, bringing it back to its original appearance and returning the plastering to its old color. The cloister has been used to display exhibits since 1889, but the transfer of some sculptures to Palazzo Massimo alle Terme and Palazzo Altemps has modified the layout and new works have been set up in their place. Numerous statues, stelae and sarcophagi are arranged in the four wings; many of these are noteworthy works that illustrate the requirements of a middle- to upper-class clientele who wished to present an image in keeping with their social status. There are too many of them for us to mention more than the most significant. Other statues are located in the garden, for the most part colossal heads of animals (not all of them dating from antiquity) from Palazzo Valentini (near Trajan's Column), where they were found in 1586.

The central fountain and the colossal heads of animals around it.

Wing I

Wing I houses some important sculptures: the headless statue wearing a lorica (mail shirt) found on the Via Praenestina, a statue of a man in heroic seminudity from San Giovanni Incarico and the beautiful 2nd-century-AD statue of a standing woman, probably a priestess of Ceres, holding ears of grain and poppies, i.e. the attributes of the goddess. The pair of seated headless statues from the Julio-Claudian period in the middle of the wing are of outstanding quality: coming from a sepulchral monument at Tor Pignattara, one is of a man dressed in a toga and the other of a draped woman, derived from a type used in the Hellenistic era for images of Tychai and of Muses. Of particular interest among the funeral altars and sarcophagi on dis-

play are the altar of T. Aspulenus Carellianus, decorated with a rich series of funerary decorative motifs, and the sarcophagus of a child with a *Centauromachy* on the chest and a *Gigantomachy* on the lid.

Wing II

Wing II presents a wide variety of sarcophagi and allows us to appreciate the full range of their decorative repertoire. In many cases they are adorned with Dionysiac scenes in which the god is accompanied by a procession of satyrs and bacchantes (while the discovery of the sleeping Ariadne is depicted on the sarcophagus found in the church of Santi Nereo e Achilleo). On others we find the scheme of two winged figures holding an inscription or clipeus (medallion) with the bust of the deceased: on the 3rd-century-AD sarcophagus found on the Via Casilina two winged genii hold the clipeus, while beneath them are set Oceanus and Tellus and the image of the centaur Chiron educating Achilles is repeated on the sides. Among the sarcophagi with mythological scenes is one from Palazzo Caucci, just after the middle of the wing, illustrating the myth of Medea, from the dispatch of poisoned gifts to Creusa to her flight, after killing her sons, on the chariot drawn by dragons. A series of smaller sarcophagi belong to children and are usually decorated with erotes as a reminder of their youth. At the end of the wing are set two imposing sarcophagi from the late 1st century AD that depict their owners lying on their funeral beds (*klini*).

Wing III

A series of altars and bases of statues that were dedicated to numerous deities and the genius of the emperor by the *equites singulares* (imperial horse guards) at the time of their discharge are located at the beginning of Wing III. They are followed by funerary altars, some of them adorned with figurative decorations like the small altar depicting the brothers Biton and Cleobis taking the place of the oxen to pull their mother's cart all the way to Delphi. After these come numerous funerary reliefs with portraits of the deceased and some statues, including a sleeping boy with a hood holding a lantern inspired by Hellenistic genre sculpture and a statue of a women holding an idol with Archaic traits. The elegant funerary relief representing a centaur carrying off a nymph comes from the Via Praenestina, while next to it is set the remarkable headless statue of Aphrodite standing, belonging to the type known as the Venus Callipyge.

Relief from the Via Praenestina with a centaur carrying off a nymph.

Wing IV

Wing IV houses a number of portraits and works of ideal sculpture, copies and reworkings of Greek statues used as idols for worship and more frequently to decorate gardens, houses, villas and public buildings. There are numerous gods like Dionysius (represented drunk and leaning on a pillar from which hangs a goatskin), Aphrodite, Hera and Diana, whose cult is also illustrated by two decorated altars dedicated to the goddess. In the middle of the wing, the statue representing an elderly fisherman is a Roman copy inspired by models

A wing of Michelangelo's Cloister.

developed in the Hellenistic era by the "realistic" current active chiefly in Alexandria. A short distance away stands a small statuary group with Ganymede and Jupiter's eagle perched on a rock. Unusual are the "sofa" capital on which two boys are seated and the small votive sculpture representing a ship surmounted by the base of a column, probably vowed by a sailor for his return. At the end of the wing it is worth singling out two statues of Hercules, one standing and one seated, inspired by the models of Polyclitus, and one of an athlete from the Via Ostiensis. Onto this wing faces the inner part of the first door of the cloister, decorated with an oil painting of the Carthusian monk Foulquois, executed by Filippo Balbi in 1855. Father of Pope Clement IV, Foulquois took vows after losing his wife and died in 1265. (M.C.)

The door painted
with a picture of the
Carthusian monk Foulquois.

The Archeological Tour

It is also possible to take an archeological tour of the Museo delle Terme, visiting the surviving ancient buildings of the complex constructed by Diocletian. Some of these have been incorporated into Santa Maria degli Angeli e dei Martiri, where the apse of the *caldarium* (on the façade), the *tepidarium* and the large *frigidarium* can be recognized. The church of San Bernardo is also built in one of the circular rooms of the outer enclosure. On the other hand some of the Aule delle Olearie, or Oil Warehouses, the largest public work carried out by Clement XIII in order to ensure an efficient supply of oil to Rome, are part of the museum; they stand to the right of the Basilica of Santa Maria degli Angeli. Finally the museum also includes the so-called Octagonal Hall and the adjacent Hall of Sant'Isidoro.

The latter is a small square room roofed with a cross vault that was annexed to the granary called the Annona in 1640, before being converted in 1754 into the chapel of Sant'Isidoro in Thermis, of which only the façade remains today. The series of large halls (I-XI) of the Baths has been part of the museum since 1911, when the great archeological exhibition was staged there in 1911. Except for Hall X, they are used today for temporary exhibitions, while awaiting a definitive solution.definitivo.

Hall X

Hall X, belonging to the surviving part of the Baths of Diocletian that has been incorporated into the museum, has recently been restored and reorganized to house some important funerary monuments. It was probably originally used as an atrium providing access to Hall IX, once an *apodyterium* (changing room). On the left as you enter stands the massive structure from the Julio-Claudian period known as the Tomb of the Platorini, discovered on the right bank of the Tiber in 1880 and reconstructed for the Archeological Exhibition of 1911. The tomb is preceded by the statues found inside it: the one of a man in heroic nudity, traditionally identified as G. Sulpicius Platorinus, may actually be a portrait of Marcus Artorius Geminus, the probable builder of the tomb around 20 AD, while the statue of a woman may be of its last owner, Antonia Furnilla, who lived in Nero's reign. Inside the cinerary urns have been put back in the places where they were found. The fine bust of Minatia Polla, Artorius Geminus's wife also comes from the tomb. On the opposite side of the

Statue of man in heroic nudity, probably representing M. Artorius Geminus.

hall are the two chamber tombs uncovered in 1951 in the area of the large necropolis on the Via Portuensis and transferred to the Museo Nazionale Romano after a complex intervention to cut them out of the tuff in which they were carved. One tomb has a rich painted decoration (see p. 60), while the other, dated to the beginning of the 3rd century AD, is adorned with extremely refined stuccoes. The small chamber, enlivened by niches and roofed with a tunnel vault, contained a set of decorations with an allegorical meaning, characterized by mythological figures set in the medallions of the vault (Dioscuri, satyrs, nymphs and erotes). The opposite wall is adorned instead with two erotes, floral motifs and a syrinx, the wind instrument played by shepherds. Also on display in the hall are several funeral statues, located in the niches, a number of sarcophagi arranged along the walls, including the beautiful one representing the myth of Dionysius and Ariadne found on the Via Labicana. Standing out, finally, for its rarity

is the smaller than life-size equestrian statue of a boy that is one of the few examples of the use of one of the most prestigious types of Roman statuary for the burial of a child.

The entrance to the former planetarium.

The Octagonal Hall
The Octagonal Hall is part of the central complex of the Baths of Diocletian and the last of the four rooms that were located next to the *caldarium* and that were converted into a store for Rome's grain supply in 1575, eventually becoming, in 1764, part of the storehous-

es for oil (the "Olearie"). The first two halls also survive in part and now house the Faculty of Education, while Via Cernaia cuts through the third. The fourth hall is square on the outside and octagonal on the inside (with semicircular niches in the corners) and may have been used as the baths' secondary *frigidarium*, judging by the fact that it contained a hexagonal basin up until the 16th century. The present floor is the result of the papal interventions that subdivided the hall into three stories. The "umbrella" dome is still the original one, while the stucco decoration of the ceiling and the marble decoration of the walls have been lost. The hall was used for the great Archeological Exhibition of 1911, but then turned first into a cinema (Sala Minerva) and then a planetarium (1928), the largest in Europe at the time. It was not until 1991 that the building was restructured and used to display sculptures found in baths, in order to give these works back their original function in a similar setting to the one for which they were intended. Today it is used for exhibitions as well. The statues on show also give us an idea of the subjects portrayed in baths, chiefly images of athletes, heroes and deities. They formed complex decorative programs that unfortunately cannot be reconstructed today. Among the statues from the Baths of Diocletian themselves it is worth mentioning the copy of Praxiteles's *Aphrodite of Cnidus*, a remarkable man's torso, copy of a classical original, and the beautiful head of a young athlete from the time of Hadrian, copy of an original in the severe style. From the Baths of Caracalla come two copies of works by Polyclitus (a torso of the *Doryphorus* and the statue of *Heracles*) and a fine statue of *Aphrodite Anadyomene* ("Rising From the Sea"), shown wringing the water from her hair, that was found in the Mithraeum under the baths. Several heads, like that of Asclepius and one of a youth wearing a diadem, also come from Caracalla's Baths, while a pair of herms of Apollo and Hermes probably decorated their library. Finally a copy of Praxiteles's *Lycian Apollo* was found in the Baths of Trajan. (M.C.)

View of the interior of the Octagonal Hall with sculptures from thermal baths.

The Painted Tomb from Via Portuensis

The tomb, carved in tuff and with an approximately rectangular plan, must have belonged to a well-to-do family that used it together with their freedmen. In fact it has a total of 26 niches for the ashes of the cremated in the walls and six spaces for interments. Its painted decoration diverges from the more customary choices in 2nd-century-AD tombs, in which the preference was to rely on the allegorical meaning of mythological scenes as a defense against death. In the decoration of the tomb from the Via Portuensis, dating from around the middle of the century, a more "popular" approach was taken in which symbolic significance was assigned to images drawn from everyday life. In the two lateral tympana of the central wall are set portraits of two young men inserted in medallions, while at bottom right we see a seated couple, probably the parents of the two youths who had died before their time. On the entrance wall is set a scene of a conjugal banquet, while on the ceiling we can recognize the seasons and a scene of a boat landing on a shore; on the left-hand wall three rows of niches are surmounted a pair of peacocks facing one another. In the middle of the wall on the right, devoid of niches, is located the oldest part of the decorative program: here in fact we can see, from the right and under two garlands, three groups of young adults (men and women) playing games: two pairs of men and women engaged excitedly in a ballgame, a youth covering his eyes while a companion flees and a woman seems be holding him back (perhaps it is a game of hide-and-seek rather than blind-man's-buff, in which a blindfold is worn) and finally more young people are seated or lying down, engaged in pleasant conversation or in another game. On the left advances the solitary and out-of-scale figure of a child who is probably learning to walk by playing with a three-wheeled cart. It is likely that the at once familiar and playful scenes on this wall expressed the hope that the afterlife (in the Elysian Fields?) would carry on in a manner not too different from the happy and carefree moments in everyday life, perfectly embodied by this little "catalogue" of games, played by children and grownups. If, however, the child depicted on his own was the deceased commemorated, then they may also have been an allusion to the joys denied him by the brevity of his life. (M.C.)

Frescoes of people playing games from a painted tomb on the Via Portuensis.

Bibliography

N. Horsfall, *CIL VI 37965 = CLE 1988 Epitaph of Allia Potestas: a commentary*, in "ZPE", 1985, pp. 251-272.

F. Silvestrini, *Sepulcrum Marci Artori Gemini. La tomba detta dei Platorini nel Museo Nazionale Romano*, Roma 1987.

M. Rita Sanzi di Mino (ed. by), *Rotunda Diocletiani. Sculture decorative delle terme nel Museo Nazionale Romano*, Roma 1991.

Fidene. Una casa dell'età del ferro, Milano 1998.

S. De Maria, *Le tombeau de la via Portuense à Rome*, in N. Blanc (ed. by), *Au royaume des ombres. La peinture funéraire antique* (exhibition catalogue, Saint-Romain-en-Gal, Vienne 1998), Paris 1998, pp. 126-130.

A.M. Bietti Sestieri, A. De Santis, *Protostoria dei popoli latini: Museo nazionale romano, Terme di Diocleziano*, Milano 2000.

L. Nista (ed. by), *Sacellum Herculis. Le sculture del tempio di Ercole a Trastevere*, Roma 1991.

R. Friggeri, *La collezione epigrafica del Museo Nazionale Romano alle Terme di Diocleziano*, Milano 2001.

Museo Nazionale Romano. Terme di Diocleziano, Milano 2002.

Cover and graphics
Tassinari/Vetta

Translation
Christopher Evans

This volume was printed for Mondadori Electa S.p.A.
by Mondadori Printing S.p.A.,Verona, in 2012